THE

ROAD

TO

JOY

A Lent-to-Easter Devotional
from Christianity Today

Introduction

THE DAYS LEADING TO THE RESURRECTION of Jesus
Christ (the Lenten season) are some of the most significant of the year
for many Christians in a variety of theological traditions. Whereas
the Advent season is celebrated as a time of joyful anticipation, Lent
is traditionally practiced with a sense of sober observance, charac-
terized by repentance, self-denial, and an awareness of our sinful
humanity that led to Christ's atonement of our sins. While it is right
and good for Christians to enter into a time of somber reflection as
we look to the Cross, we don't want to forget that this is a road with
a joyful conclusion—the resurrection of Christ.

For this Easter and Lenten season, we will begin a journey down
The Road to Joy.

The imagery of a road can evoke visions of sun-drenched stretches
through the desert, tree-lined paths through the woods, or lonely high-
ways traveling through the middle of nowhere. As we journey onward,
we are met with numerous challenges as we get closer to our desired
destination, but we press on courageously, convinced that it will have
been worth it when we reach the end.

In some ways, this echoes our salvation stories, where we experience the sobering yet sanctifying reality of Christ's death in our lives
while never losing sight of the hopeful joy that his resurrecting power
provides as we draw nearer to him, our desired destination. I pray that
as you spend time reading and meditating on these hopeful reflections, your heart will be freshly renewed as you remember the one
who endured the Cross, for the joy that was set before him.

– Ronnie Martin

Contents

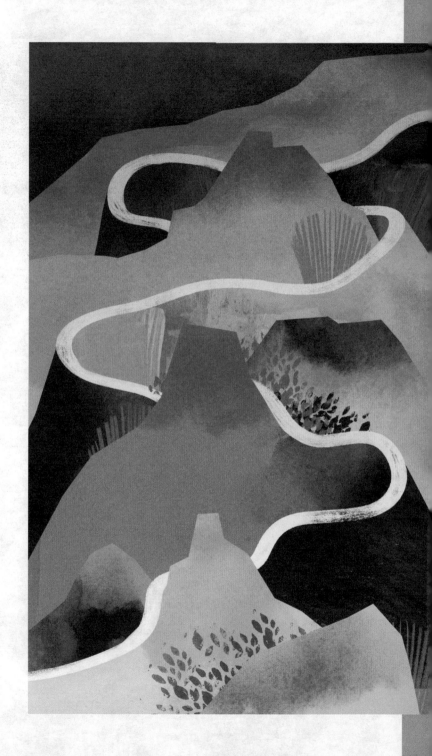

reflections on
LENT

"O Lord, make me know
my end and what is the
measure of my days; let me
know how fleeting I am!"

PSALM 39:4 (ESV)

Our Fragility

———

HE
REMEMBERS
OUR FRAMES

By Zack Eswine

Psalm 103:14

IN EDEN, EVERYTHING WAS A HALLELUJAH. *Good! Very good!* God said (Gen. 1:1-31). Though brown and gray, even dust was a dappled speck of glittering life. Grand as the mountains. Majestic like whales. For even the tiniest fleck which clung to the hidden underside of Adam and Eve's broom was cherished and celebrated, a treasured gift from God (Prov. 8:26).

Have you ever seen a snow-laden valley blanketed in soft white? When untouched and gleaming in the sunlight, before any human boot has pressed its mud-mixed imprint into it? In Eden, dust was associated with untouched beauty like this. All gleaming light. No muddy boot.

However, when David writes this psalm, he is a long way from Eden and innocence. His sins are many. He'd been sinned against too. He was dust. Not innocent and colorful, but what dust had become. Like all other created goods, dust was now twinged by death. Dingy, the dignity of its tiny fleck in Eden was gone. In the fallen world, tiny flecks are flicked. No one sees dust, and if one does, he tries to rid his room of it.

> For out of it you were taken;
> for you are dust,
> and to dust you shall return. (Gen. 3:19, ESV)

Dust was once Edenic (out of it you were taken). Now dust signals death (to dust you shall return).

When we sin as David had, we wonder about how God remembers us. Will God forget the dignity he gave us, or remembering our frailty, will he shun or abandon us?

In Psalm 103, David describes God as one who remembers and who is merciful and gracious (Ps. 103:4, 8). God is slow to anger and abounding with steadfast love, the kind of love no one can take from us (Ps. 103:4, 8, 11, 17).

As one who remembers, God banishes condemnation when we repent. Look to any horizon in any direction, and all a sinner will see is the shining light of the forgiveness of God (Ps. 103:11-12).

IN THIS WORLD, IT IS NOT DEATH THAT IS STEADFAST BUT DIVINE LOVE.

For God is like the most compassionate father (Ps. 103:13). Slow to anger, merciful, gracious, abounding with love, this Father is delighted when remembering the dignity of the one he loves. Such a Father would never give a scorpion or snake to one dearly loved who needs an egg or bread (Luke 11:11-13). On the contrary, such a compassionate Father would use his bold strength to gently brace, fiercely protect, and sacrificially guard the vulnerable child he loves. As a compassionate father who is good, God remembers our frame. He remembers that we are dust.

Whenever I've been with parents as they hold their little or grown children in their children's last moments on this earth, compassionate and loving parents cradle them, speaking words of lifelong love. They remember their loved one's frame. They cry, in Jesus, declaring the existence of a love that somehow overcomes even this death of deaths.

By faith, they know that it is not the Grim Reaper who comes for their loved one. It is the God who created and remembers their child that comes.

It is not death winning in those last breaths but death taking its last stand.

Remember, in this world, it is not death that is steadfast but divine love.

This divine love, mentioned four times in this psalm, remembers not only that we are dust in death, but also that it was with dust he had given us life.

He knows our frame. He remembers.

So when ash is smeared on our foreheads today, we confront a difficult truth. Death as dust is a scene in our story that we cannot escape. Sorrows for sins against us. Repentance for our own contribution.

And yet, in Christ Jesus, death as dust has never been and will never be the truest thing about us. Death has an enemy. his name is Jesus Christ.

When we receive ashes on our heads today, we declare by faith that death will die. Because death could not hold Jesus in the grave, dust will rise again, recovered to the glory given it in Eden and all the more in the new kingdom that awaits us.

This is why when the earliest followers of Jesus thought of death, they declare it their last enemy (1 Cor. 15:26). They learned to see this enemy outflanked at every turn by God's steadfast love in Christ Jesus, from which nothing, not even death, can separate us (Rom. 8:38-39).

Our God is our great rememberer. He remembers our frames, that we are dust. Held by him, we hope. ◼

———

IF
ANYONE
WOULD
COME

By Jeremy Linneman

Matthew 16:24

THE ROAD TO JOY, FOR JESUS, ran through Jerusalem. It was a path of self-denial, sacrifice, and death—before it was the passage into joy, redemption, and glory.

So it is for all who would follow in his steps. To walk with Jesus is to take the way of the Cross. To enter his kingdom is to knowingly and willingly choose the joy of self-denial.

How can we say the "joy" of self-denial? True joy doesn't take the long way around pain; it doesn't take a shortcut toward glory. True joy moves through hardship. True joy goes with Jesus through Jerusalem. The way is narrow, and the gate is small, but freedom and joy await the disciple who stays on the path.

Jesus said, "Whoever wants to be my disciple must deny themselves and take up their cross and follow me" (Matt. 16:24). This is rightly understood to be one of Jesus' most intimidating challenges. But it is also one of his most subversive invitations. "Get off the road that leads to death," he's saying. "Choose instead this unexpected way to the good life—through denying and dying to self."

Indeed, our denial is an essential step in becoming like Jesus. Dallas Willard wrote that "a shift toward self-denial is needed to reorder the . . . human self in subordination to God. . . .

Christian spiritual formation rests on this indispensable foundation of death to self and cannot proceed except insofar as that foundation is being firmly laid and sustained." What is the self-life that is being denied and laid down? It is the old self which needs to be put off. It is the old life that wasn't so appealing anyway. To deny ourselves and follow Jesus is the most freeing and wonderful thing; it is to let go of what wasn't working in the first place. The new, selfless life that takes its place is the truly good life—a new heart devoted to God, a life of honesty, vulnerability, acceptance, friendship, communion, and purpose.

YET IN THIS TENSION OF CHALLENGE AND INVITATION, REMEMBER WHO SUPPLIES THE STRENGTH AND WISDOM FOR A LIFE OF SELF-DENIAL. IT IS JESUS.

To be sure, self-denial is not the same as self-rejection. Self-rejection occurs when the soul says to itself, "See, everyone was right. I'm an awful person. I'm a failure and a mistake." Self-rejection also says, "I am not so secure in myself, so I must rise and prove myself, must fight and defend myself." This is not the way of Jesus, and it's not self-denial. It is a rejection of what God has made and declared good.

How do we know when we are practicing self-rejection and not self-denial? Self-rejection leads to shame, hiding, and self-criticism. It also makes us critical and demanding toward others. (We're critical of others when we believe God is critical toward us.)

Self-denial, on the other hand, leads to a joyful submission to the Father. It is the freedom to reject the ways of the world—its anger, greed, and envy. Self-denial is an active choice to become like Jesus in his radical inner simplicity and wholehearted devotion to the Father. It is what the late Tim Keller called a "blessed self-forgetfulness."

And unlike self-rejection, self-denial frees us to love and serve others purely. (We're merciful toward others when we believe God is merciful toward us.)

Self-denial, then, is both the most difficult thing in the Christian life and the simplest. Laying down our lives can't happen just once; it's a complete surrender we make moment by moment, every day. Only if we truly embrace Jesus' self-denying, non-defensive death on the cross can we believe we are accepted into his Father's delight.

Yet in this tension of challenge and invitation, remember who supplies the strength and wisdom for a life of self-denial. It is Jesus. He provides all we need to follow in his self-giving love—namely, his Spirit. As we abide in him, walking by his Spirit, we come out with complete joy (John 15:11).

In a world consumed with earning, showing, and defending, self-denial seems like a radical and dangerous thing. But in the right-side-up kingdom of Jesus, it is the safest, simplest, and happiest place. In him, we lack nothing and have everything. Will you receive it? Will you deny yourself, take up your cross, and follow Jesus into full and eternal joy?

Lord Jesus, thank you that you are with me. I did not choose you, but you chose me and appointed me to die to myself and take up your life. Grant me your strength and wisdom to choose this life, not just once, but every moment. My life is yours. Lead me, by your Spirit and your self-giving love, into everlasting joy. ■

I HAVE CALMED AND QUIETED MY SOUL

By John Starke

Psalm 131

IN OUR LIFE WITH GOD IN THIS WORLD, we often need to sit quietly and be honest with ourselves. What worries and anxieties are occupying our minds and governing our behavior more than they should? Sitting quietly is difficult. We don't like what happens when we do. All the ghosts and goblins from below, which we have so effectively silenced in the hurry of each day, suddenly come to the surface. When we are still, we often scroll. We scroll through algorithms available to us for the silencing of the inner panic. But when we resist the scrolling, we are often left with lingering pains, insecurities, and thoughts that worry us and, more than we realize, control us.

While we may be effective at managing our interior lives, our management never leads to healing. At best we can numb our pain with our distractions, but the Book of Psalms offers a different path. In the presence of the Lord, we acknowledge these pains and worries, allowing them to come to the surface. The good news, however, is that the Lord never brings things to the surface that he doesn't intend to heal.

"Oh Lord, my heart is not lifted up; my eyes are not raised too high; I do not occupy myself with things too great and too marvelous for me" (Ps. 131:1, ESV).

There are many things we can offer up to the Lord and say, "This is too much. Only you can carry me through." There are a lot of things that shouldn't concern us, and worrying about them never makes things better. It only diminishes us. Jesus gives us examples of worrying about money, possessions, and what tomorrow may bring (Matt. 6:34). But even more, I wonder if we might need to offer to God the management of our interior lives and emotional entanglements. There might be wounds from friends, intimates, and family that linger and torment us, creating a sustained inner dialogue that simply rehearses the pain over and over. There might be moments of humiliation and failure at work or in our marriages that make us shrink back and cringe at ourselves. Our management strategies haven't brought healing or resolve, only lingering pain, and like cancer, the wounds only grow and fester.

GROWING IN SPIRITUAL MATURITY REQUIRES REMEMBERING WE HAVE NEVER GONE WITHOUT CARE AND ATTENTION FROM GOD.

Let us sit quietly with the Lord, being honest with him and ourselves, saying, "Oh Lord, I recognize I don't have what it takes to heal these wounds. They control me more than I control them. They are too great for me."

"But I have calmed and quieted my soul, like a weaned child with its mother; like a weaned child is my soul within me" (Ps. 131:2, ESV).

For an infant, dependent upon a mother's milk, every meal is an emergency, every hunger pang a panic. Only after the consistent experience of being fed, never going without care and attention, does a child learn that when hunger comes, it's going to be okay. Food has always come, and it will come again. The infant can sit in her mother's lap without groping and grasping because she has grown an instinct of being settled, even when the feelings of neediness and hunger arise.

While an infant grows an instinct of being settled, we must be intentional about it. "But I have calmed and quieted my soul." I am intentionally seeking God's presence, taking a deep breath, and remembering all the times he has been my help. As an infant cannot feed herself, neither can we appropriately heal our wounds and emotional entanglements. Our management strategies have left us like unweaned children, groping and grasping, anxiously seeking out ways to feel safe in this world. Every emotion is an emergency and every pain a panic. Growing in spiritual maturity requires remembering we have never gone without care and attention from God. When the pain and sadness come, it's going to be okay. The Spirit has always been near, and he will be near again.

"O Israel, hope in the Lord from this time forth and forevermore" (Ps. 131:3, ESV).

We must be honest with ourselves. At times our interior entanglements and worry have governed our lives more than we'd like to admit. We are tossed to and fro by our anxious thoughts, and our own management strategies haven't been effective. In fact, they have distanced and desensitized us from the experience of God's presence and love for our healing and renewal. Let us seek the Lord, opening ourselves to him, hoping not in our self-management but in his presence and power. From this time forth and forevermore, lay your management strategies and safety schemes down. Hope in the Lord and his goodness. ∎

REJOICE IN OUR SUFFERINGS

By Dan Hyun

reflections on

THE THIRD SUNDAY OF LENT

Romans 5:3-5

REJOICE IN SUFFERING. It may sound ridiculous, if not offensive, especially to those of us walking through the very real fires of life. For most, to rejoice in life means trying to remove as much of our hardship as possible. And to be clear, we shouldn't be weird people who actively pursue suffering. Life isn't some kind of bizarre spiritual CrossFit where actively punishing ourselves somehow brings us closer to God.

Still, one of the most astounding implications of dwelling with Jesus is that we can now view our suffering through a new set of eyes. It may honestly feel like a mystery that takes the whole journey of life to fully unpack. But when suffering occurs—and for all of us it's not an if but a when—we recognize God's invitation to enjoy his very real presence with us.

Paul was writing to a people like us who experienced the hard things of life—a people who faced the sort of challenges leading them to understandably question all these wonderful doctrines of salvation that Paul had written about. Like some of us may ask, "If we're really doing all this gospel-centered life right, should life be this hard?"

Paul's reply: actually, yes.

Part of working out our salvation is growing in awareness of the Lord's presence. Absolutely in those moments when we'd naturally expect to feel his presence, times of sweet communion or satisfying moments of ministry when there's absolutely no doubt that God really loves us. It's right to savor and enjoy God in those times, but not just in those times.

IT'S IMPORTANT TO RECOGNIZE THAT THE NATURE OF HOPE IS THAT WE DON'T YET HAVE WHAT WE'RE LONGING FOR.

Working out the profound implications of Good News is learning to trust the presence of Christ with us in all things—even those horrible things that keep us up at night drowning in the sorrow of helpless tears.

Again, we don't celebrate suffering itself. Rather, we boast "in" our afflictions. That's a critical distinction. We're not masochists who think pain itself is good. May we be compassionate people who grieve with those who suffer very real pain. Because into that grief, we can also offer real hope. Hope that even if we may never fully understand the "why" of suffering—at least on this side of glory—knowing the "who" invites us to trust in God's character. To trust that there is a divine meaning to the hard things we endure, meaning that even lets us rejoice believing that we are being shaped to reflect his good glory to our world.

Our suffering produces endurance. As a runner training for a marathon has to believe, those grueling practice runs are building endurance for the race. Knowing your aim can help give meaning to what may feel like torture.

And this endurance produces character. I chuckle when newlywed couples offer marriage advice. Not that it's unhelpful, but there is a weight girding the wisdom offered by couples who've endured through long, hard years together and come out stronger. Character isn't developed like heating up a quick dish in the microwave; it requires the slow cooker of life that sometimes doesn't even look like it's cooking.

And demonstrated character then leads to hope. It's important to recognize that the nature of hope is that we don't yet have what we're longing for.

Persevering in hope can make you feel silly, but this journey of hope grows our trust in who God is. Even as it feels like so many other promises of our world ultimately disappoint, God will never let you down.

This isn't just sweetly sentimental. God's love is an on-the-ground, dirt-under-the-nails kind of presence. It's the demonstrated love of a Savior suffering on a real cross that speaks hope into the darkest of places.

It's the kind of hope where you discover that even if everything else in this world feels like it's against you, God is for you, and that's enough.

In the countercultural ways of God, suffering isn't just something to be endured, but the mystery of his loving hands forming us in beauty. Trust that God loves you like this, and even if your hands are trembling, rejoice in your suffering. ◼

Our Remembrance

———

IN THE RUSH OF GREAT WATERS

By Heather Thompson Day

Psalm 32

MANY YEARS AGO, I had a student who shared with our class that he had killed a motorcyclist in a car accident.

I was teaching a creative writing class. Every class period, we opened by looking at a writing prompt that I had projected onto the large screen. One evening every week, students would come in and quietly unzip their backpacks. You didn't hear voices, just the quiet scratches of pen on paper. It is a sound that we don't hear much of in classrooms anymore. Every week, the large white screen revealed a different prompt. One week it said, "They never noticed me, but I noticed them." Another week it read, "Of all the things I have learned, this was the most important."

We got to know each other well in that classroom. Students who thought they were terrible writers discovered the power of their own voices. We learned from the lives of one another. We grew one pen scratch at a time.

One week in particular, the prompt read,

"Do you forgive me?" That's when my student read to the class his story of a car accident that was his fault, where he killed a motorcyclist. He told us that the experience destroyed him. He dropped out of school. He developed severe depression. He pulled away from friends and family and spent nearly two years in isolation and self-loathing.

Psalm 32:3-4 encapsulates how he was feeling. "When I kept silent, my bones wasted away through my groaning all day long. For day and night your hand was heavy on me; my strength was sapped as in the heat of summer."

THIS LENT, MAY WE ALL APPROACH THE REMEMBRANCE OF THE CROSS WITH THE HEART OF MY STUDENT.

He went on to tell us that his life was changed by an unexpected display of forgiveness. He wrote a letter to the parents of the man he had killed. He expressed his sorrow for the accident and shared how grieved he had been by their loss.

Psalm 32:5 reads, "Then I acknowledged my sin to you and did not cover up my iniquity. I said, 'I will confess my transgressions to the Lord.' And you forgave the guilt of my sin." That is exactly what the parents who had buried their son did. They wrote my student a letter and forgave him for the accident, but that wasn't all they did. The letter included an invitation. They invited my student to join them for dinner. They gave him the seat of the son they had lost. They made him a meal. They showed him pictures. They told him stories of the boy they had loved. And in this unbelievable act of compassion and kindness, my student found grace and healing.

Psalm 32:1-2 reads, "Blessed is the one whose transgressions are forgiven, whose sins are covered. Blessed is the one whose sin the Lord does not count against them."

My student would return every year to have dinner with the parents of the man he had killed. And every year, they would open their home, and their memories, and offer my student forgiveness.

I have never forgotten this story. It is one of the clearest examples I have seen of the image of God in the image bearers of God. The sacrifice of these parents changed the life of my student forever. They lost one son and yet found the strength to redeem someone else's. He went back to school. He found a therapist. He experienced the healing and restoration to his life that being washed from sin through grace always offers those of us who know the depths of which we need it.

This Lent, may we all approach the remembrance of the Cross with the heart of my student. I hope you remember the God who has remembered you. I hope you will accept the grace that has been freely given.

Psalm 32:10 says, "But the LORD's unfailing love surrounds the one who trusts in him."

My prompt that day that was projected on a giant white screen said, "Do you forgive me?" This Easter season, may we all remember how Christ gave his life in answer to that question. "Yes," the Lord responded. And then he hung his head and died. The church has been living ever since. ■

Our Endurance

NOR
BE
WEARY

By Jeremy Writebol

Hebrews 12:5-7

I'VE RIDDEN A BICYCLE across the state of North Carolina. Twice. Mostly.

In full disclosure, we didn't cross the entire state. In fact, a good chunk of the ride was in South Carolina, but that's beside the point. Two days on each trek. Up and down the rolling hills of the Carolina Piedmont on the way to the coast. One hundred and fifty miles on a heavy, iron-framed, used bicycle in the sweltering humidity and heat of mid-September. It was unbearable and nearly physically broke me. But we did it.

My father had (for reasons that remain unknown and mysterious to me) decided that it would be a great bonding exercise for him, myself, and my younger brother. We were going to support a national nonprofit organization's fundraising efforts by riding in their 150-mile event. He enrolled us and promised it would be a lot of fun and push us to do something significant together. Looking back, he was right. But the fun and the significance of it, even 30 years later, is also remembered alongside the agony.

To be able to ride a bike 150 miles in the course of two days requires significant stamina and energy. It's not a thing that most of us can get up in the morning and decide on a whim to do that day. It requires preparation, training, and—dare I say—discipline. So Dad took my brother and me out on longer and longer training rides through the hot summer to train our bodies. They weren't optional. They weren't fun. These training rides were discipline, but they developed a capacity and an ability to actually enjoy 150 miles of biking to the beach.

> "THE LORD DISCIPLINES THE ONE HE LOVES, AND HE CHASTENS EVERYONE HE ACCEPTS AS HIS SON."

The 40 days of Lent are a slog for people like me who are used to the instant gratification and immediate reward lifestyle of our current culture. Yet the effort of observing a season of repentance, prayer, fasting, and almsgiving to increase my affections for Jesus is worth it. Just like my father's grueling training rides, enduring under a set of disciplines for a season prepares us for greater joy at the Resurrection. They may even help us find greater joy in the here and now as we journey by faith to the New Jerusalem.

The writer of Hebrews understands the dynamic of our need for discipline and the Father's good and holy purposes for us. We're encouraged to not disregard or belittle the processes and practices of discipline God puts us under. When corrected, even rebuked, we're encouraged not to grow weary of the process of formation. Ultimately, the application is for us to "endure hardship as discipline" (Heb. 12:7). The discipline of God is for our good, and to avoid, spurn, or reject his careful formation of us is to circumvent becoming like Christ.

Yet there is more to discipline than just getting better or stronger. Enduring the hardship and correction the Lord places us under is a sign of a unique identity we have from God. Hebrews 12:6-7 tells us, "The Lord disciplines the one he loves, and he chastens everyone he accepts as his son . . . God is treating you as his children." When we experience the hardship of spiritual discipline and correction, we're really experiencing the loving training and formation of the Father. We're not prison inmates being punished for our crimes, nor unruly students being barked at by an uncaring teacher. We're beloved children being shaped into mature saints, able to experience surprising resilience and sustained joy until we are together with our Father forever.

Biking to the beach, and all the training rides along with it, built a lasting memory with and affection for my father, even if it took blood, sweat, and tears—the stuff of enduring hardship—to attain. The hardship and discipline from our heavenly Father will build a lasting capacity for joy and eternal delight when he brings us home. Don't lose heart, nor be weary. ◾

"Out of the depths I
cry to you, O Lord!
O Lord, hear my voice!
Let your ears be
attentive to the voice of
my pleas for mercy!"

PSALM 130:1-2 (ESV)

meditations on
HOLY WEEK

HAVE THIS MIND AMONG YOURSELVES

By Barnabas Piper

meditations on
PALM SUNDAY

———

Philippians 2:5-11

PALM SUNDAY CELEBRATES the triumphal entry of Jesus into Jerusalem, riding on a donkey and being regaled with praise by the masses. To call it that, though, demands that we know how the story ends. Jesus was riding to his betrayal, false imprisonment, and torturous death. On the face of it, there is little that is "triumphant" about that, but this is how Jesus always works in accordance with his Father's plan. The glory (or triumph) comes through sacrifice. Philippians 2 shows us this.

In Philippians 2:5 (ESV), believers are called to "have this mind among yourselves." What mind? That "which is yours in Christ Jesus." Paul doesn't tell us what our shared mind and perspective should be like. Rather, he describes Jesus to us, because it is in him that we have this mind (perspective, thought process, values, beliefs). So let's consider Jesus together.

Jesus set aside equality with God. He did not cling to his rightful status as over and above all. This doesn't mean he gave up his deity but that he voluntarily became unglorified and unheavenly. He went the opposite direction of every human instinct; we cling to whatever status and power we have. (Why do you think HOA presidents, school librarians, and assistant retail managers can be such tyrants? Why do you think we so readily yell at our kids?) We won't relinquish reputation for anything. He released his willingly.

In setting aside his rightful status, Jesus emptied himself of glory and became a servant. Serving is weakness. Serving is invisible. Serving is a job we relegate to those who are "unskilled" or considered lower in society, even if we are too genteel to say it that way. We seek glory and to be associated with the powerful. We yearn for fame, whether that is a few hours of going viral on social media or professional success. We name-drop and airbrush stories to enhance our reputations. Jesus did the opposite; he reversed the way we are to designate value, and he did so because he is the definer and giver of all true glory. In the economy of God's kingdom that Jesus ushered in, the last shall be first and the poor in spirit are blessed.

IN THE ECONOMY OF GOD'S KINGDOM THAT JESUS USHERED IN, THE LAST SHALL BE FIRST AND THE POOR IN SPIRIT ARE BLESSED.

Jesus did all this by fully, wholeheartedly, joyfully submitting to his Father's will. It is easy to think, because of our own sinful limitations, that God's plan was foisted on Jesus or that Jesus drudgingly stepped into the role of rescuing servant in order to save humanity. That is not the case at all. From before the world began, for all eternity, Jesus and the Father have been of one mind and heart. When Jesus set aside his status and glory and power, He did so "for the joy set before him" (Heb. 12:2). He did so in order to glorify the Father (John 17:4). And he did so in order to save sinners who could not save themselves (Rom. 5:8).

Here we see the beautiful backwardness of God's kingdom—or maybe it's more true to say that we see how God's kingdom upends our broken backwardness. Through humility, Jesus was glorified. Because he set aside status, the Father put him on the throne. Because he laid down his life for the world, one day the world will bow before him in reverence. Under the rule of Jesus, humility is the pathway to true glory. The triumphal entry exemplifies this. Jesus rode to the lowest, most humiliating point in all of human history, and through that came the triumph over sin and death.

Now we return to the question of "What mind?" What mind are we to have among ourselves? That which is so fixated on Jesus that we value what he values, love what he loves, and pursues what he pursued. That which is as submitted to our heavenly Father's will as his was. That which single-mindedly pursues the Father's glory as he did. That which takes joy in the glorification to come as we submit to the Father and follow Jesus. ◾

UNLESS A GRAIN OF WHEAT FALLS

By Evan Welcher

———

John 12:23-25

HOW CAN I EVER GET OVER JESUS?
I still see him from far off, ever near, always
before me, glorious glory as of the only begot-
ten, full of grace, full of truth (John 1:14).
Or rather, long did he wait, watching for me to
come home from the strange country where I
exiled myself (Luke 15:11-32).

I still don't know how to get over all this
glory or if it is wise to try. The doxa afterglow
is leading me home. He is clothed in splen-
dor, wrapped in death so as to raise us up and
never be alone. His life seemed a flash in the
pan. The limp in the hip, how I'll never forget
(Gen. 32:22-32).

God died for me to reap a harvest of
resurrection.

"The Pharisees said to one another, 'See,
this is getting us nowhere. Look how the whole
world has gone after him!'" (John 12:19).

Would that it were true.

Consider Jesus, the author of Hebrews encourages us. See him, who has endured such hostility

37

by sinners against himself, so that you will not grow weary and lose heart (Heb. 12:3).

Some Greeks asked to see Jesus, and his only reply was about death and life and the meaning of everything (John 12:20-22). How he is a kernel of wheat falling all the way into the earth to die.

Unless. But.

Unless a kernel of wheat falls to the earth and dies. But if it dies . . .

The whole world hangs on to an *if*.

How can there be joy from all this death?

A kernel of wheat must fall to the earth and die if there is to be a harvest. You, Lord, are a grain of wheat crushed to become the bread of life, and we are partakers of the bread of heaven, partakers who shall hunger no more (John 6:35).

He shall lose none of us whom the Father has given him but raise us up on the last day. This is the will of the Father (John 6:39-40).

THAT DARKNESS OF DEATH DETERRED YOU NOT. THE GLORY OF LAYING YOUR LIFE DOWN HAS LIGHTENED THE WORLD.

I have presided over 125 funerals. I saw my first wife die of cancer. Death is the stifling, smothering, mildewing darkness stalking and plaguing us all. Don't let anybody tell you any different. Don't let anybody try to sell you some saccharine bill of goods as if death doesn't matter and is of no concern. Death is the last enemy (1 Cor. 15:25-26). It is the thief of Christ's glory that comes only to steal, kill, and destroy

(John 10:10). Jesus took on death. In our place he stood con-
demned. John 12 says he is a grain of wheat falling down into
the earth. I wonder if it was dark there, in the land of death,
in the heart of the earth. Were those three days long? How
weary and lonesome love must be. Have any of us dared to
love as you have loved?

> If I ascend to heaven, You are there;
> If I make my bed in Sheol, behold, You are there.
> If I take up the wings of the dawn,
> If I dwell in the remotest part of the sea,
> Even there Your hand will lead me,
> And Your right hand will take hold of me.
> If I say, "Surely the darkness will overwhelm me,
> And the light around me will be night,"
> Even darkness is not dark to You,
> And the night is as bright as the day.
> Darkness and light are alike to You.
> (Psalm 139:8-12, NASB)

Lord Jesus, as you contemplated falling into the earth to die, did you consider that even in that shadow land, the dark would not be dark if the Father walks with us through the valley of the shadow of death? The darkness of death deterred you not. The glory of laying your life down has lightened the world. ∎

His Sorrow

EVEN
TO
DEATH

By Jamaal Williams

EVEN THE BEST OF FRIENDS sometimes fail to show up when we need them. Sometimes, they fail because we haven't expressed our needs clearly. Other times, they fail because they don't recognize the severity of our situation, are overwhelmed by their own challenges, or are preoccupied with others.

The apostle Paul, facing a death sentence at the hands of Nero, wrote to Timothy in his final letter: "At my first defense, no one came to my support, but everyone deserted me" (2 Tim. 4:16). Yet Paul, strengthened by his faith, added, "May it not be held against them." God allows his children to go through intense trials and seasons of abandonment. He uses these tests to strengthen our faith and help us see whether we trust Christ as we stumble forward, falter, or experience both.

From his words, we sense no bitterness or grudge. Instead, Paul sounds like Jesus, praying, "Father, forgive them, for they know not what they do," (Luke 23:34, ESV). While Paul's example should lead us to gratitude, Jesus' example should lead us to worship. Unlike Paul, Jesus could never say, "I am the chief of sinners," because he knew no sin.

Jesus' suffering was not just for the sake of the gospel—it was because he bore the weight of humanity's sin. And to think, Jesus willingly entered into suffering for us—for you.

What should astonish us about Jesus is that in his deepest time of need, when his closest companions—Peter, James, and John—failed to empathize with him, God's suffering servant retreated to the Father's presence like a ship seeking safe harbor in a raging storm. "In you, LORD, I have taken refuge" (Ps. 31:1) captures the essence of Jesus' prayerful retreat. Battered but anchored by faith, he paused to find the strength to continue. Jesus was exactly where God had ordained him to be: in the garden, preparing to drink the cup of God's righteous judgment for his people.

JESUS MODELS WHAT IT LOOKS LIKE TO STUMBLE INTO THE PRESENCE OF GOD—HURTING BUT HOPEFUL.

Jesus models what it looks like to stumble into the presence of God—hurting but hopeful. He approaches the Father in weakness yet displays perfect strength. Mark's gospel emphasizes Jesus' emotional suffering, describing him as "deeply distressed and troubled" and "overwhelmed with sorrow to the point of death" (Mark 14:33-34). Some view emotional suffering as sinful, but we know it's not, because Jesus—the sinless sacrifice—experienced it. Jesus cried out in faith, entrusting his pain to the Father. When we bring our anguish to God, the safest harbor, we please him.

Moreover, Jesus' anguish reveals his love for us and the weight of his task. For the joy set before him, he endured suffering. Jesus in Gethsemane teaches us how emotions, when acknowledged and submitted to God, can deepen intimacy with the Father. Emotions are like fire—they provide warmth and light when handled rightly but can become destructive when mishandled.

On this Spy Wednesday, let us marvel at our suffering servant who became our Savior by enduring the cross and its shame. May we marvel at Jesus as he leads with his "weak foot forward," encountering betrayal by his inner circle and by Judas. Judas selfishly drank from the cup of betrayal, but Jesus drank from the cup that was ordained for him alone—God's cup of wrath.

The cup Jesus was about to drink represents far more than physical suffering; it is the cup of God's righteous judgment. In the Old Testament, the "cup" symbolized God's wrath toward sin (Isa. 51:17). Jesus willingly submitted to bear that judgment for us. His agony wasn't just about the physical pain but the spiritual weight of humanity's sin. When he prayed, "Yet not what I will, but what you will" (Mark 14:36), Jesus demonstrated perfect surrender, inviting us to trust God even in our darkest moments.

As we experience loneliness and betrayal, may we resolve to trust the one who remained faithful, even to death. Like Paul, may we declare, "May it not be held against them. But the Lord stood at my side and gave me strength" (2 Tim. 4:16-17).

So how do we rely on God during deep emotional anguish? First, like Jesus, we must slow down to acknowledge the weight we are carrying. Second, make space to bring that to the Lord. Even a simple breath prayer can help at the moment, such as:

"Father, draw near to me as I draw near to you."

"Jesus, help me trust you in this moment."

"Holy Spirit, guide my thoughts and give me rest."

Set aside time for longer moments of prayer, not as an obligation to live up to, but because you have one who is always for you—even to death. Finally, pray boldly, and surrender your will boldly—the Father's heart is for you. He will hold you in his steadfast love. ■

WHEN
THE
HOUR
CAME

By Ray Ortlund

meditations on
MAUNDY THURSDAY

———

Luke 22:14-20

AT LONG LAST, Jesus came to the climactic hour for which he had been born. We rightly remember his birth with happy celebration. And we rightly remember his death with hushed reverence. We are on holy ground.

We call this day of Holy Week Maundy Thursday because of our Lord's words that evening: "A new commandment [Latin: *mandatum*] I give to you" (John 13:34, ESV).

Luke's account of the occasion points us toward two heart-melting gospel realities.

One, Jesus did not save us at a safe distance, as if by remote control. He threw himself into our salvation with wholehearted abandon. His body was shattered. His blood gushed out.

As Jesus and his disciples observed the Passover, he explained the extreme length and the profound depth of his dying love for us:

"And he took bread, and when he had given thanks, he broke it and gave it to them, saying, 'This is my body, which is given for you. Do this in remembrance of me.' And likewise the cup after they had eaten, saying, 'This cup that is poured out for you is the new covenant in my blood' " (Luke 22:19-20, ESV).

The old covenant depended, in part, on our obedience. That is why the last two words of the Old Testament are "total destruction" (Mal. 4:6). We disobeyed extremely. But our covenant betrayal did not defeat our covenant Lord. Far from backing out, he pressed in more devotedly. He sent his only Son as our all-sufficient Savior. That's why the New Testament concludes with "the grace of the Lord Jesus" (Rev. 22:21)—the final word of endless hope.

OUR RESCUING SAVIOR IS BOTH A SOLID HISTORICAL REALITY TO BE REMEMBERED AND A VIVID PRESENT EXPERIENCE TO BE SAVORED.

Let's be clear about God's covenantal arrangement with us now. We are not bringing our strengths to the table while God brings His strengths to the table so we can cobble together a team win. No, the new covenant is all of God's grace alone. And he does not lower his standards. His grace goes so far as to internalize his holy law down at the deepest substratum of our inmost beings (Heb. 8:8-13). That profound renewal is good news for everyone fed up with being "prone to wander," as the old hymn says. And Jesus sealed our new covenant hope by his very blood. He did not hold back at all.

Two, Jesus did not limit his outpouring of love to his passion and cross long ago. Yes, his atoning death was "once for all" (Heb. 7:27, ESV). To quote the *Book of Common Prayer*, he made upon the cross "by his one oblation of himself once offered, a full, perfect and sufficient sacrifice, oblation, and satisfaction for the sins of the whole world."

The finality of the Cross is the gospel message that I, as a minister, love to declare. It is the gospel we all love to hear.

But in addition, our risen Savior, through his Spirit, visits us in Holy Communion with real-time experiences of his endless grace. By calling us to eat and drink, he is saying, "My dying love for you is so real you can taste it! Come. Take it in. Be renewed."

Holy Communion is a feast. Jesus fills our hearts again and again, reassuring us that our repeated sins in this life cannot deplete his finished work on the cross.

This evening, as we receive Holy Communion in our churches, it might be like that moment in Tolkien's *Return of the King*, just after the siege of Gondor. The sound of those distant horns had declared that Rohan was coming to the rescue. Then after the battle was won, Tolkien tells us that, for Pippin, "never in after years could he hear a horn blown in the distance without tears starting in his eyes."

Our rescuing Savior is both a solid historical reality to be remembered and a vivid present experience to be savored. Tonight we will come to him as we are, with all the ruins and regrets of our sins. We will remember, with awestruck reverence, his total commitment to saving us from it all. And our eyes may well flood with tears.

"Do this in remembrance of me" invites us there. Why hold back at all? He didn't. And he doesn't. ■

His Suffering

BY
HIS
WOUNDS

By Thabiti Anyabwile

———

1 Peter 2:22-24

---

*He committed no sin, neither was deceit found in his
mouth. When he was reviled, he did not revile in return;
when he suffered, he did not threaten, but continued entrusting
himself to him who judges justly. He himself bore our sins
in his body on the tree, that we might die to sin and live to
righteousness. By his wounds you have been healed. (ESV)*

Good Friday joins together two staggering truths: "He committed no sin" and "By his wounds you have been healed."

NO SIN

Sin is so common its absence is stunning. We are a people acclimated to depravity, others' and especially our own. As soon as self-awareness dawned on us, we began a running relationship with sin. Of course, sin is not natural. Sin did not exist when God made our first parents. Adam and Eve brought sin into the world with all its power to unmake the goodness God made. Therefore, sin perverts the natural or original order of things. Sin has been so long with us that, though unnatural, it feels common. We might rightly ask ourselves, *How will we ever escape it?*

But Jesus "committed no sin." Jesus is as uncommon as sin is common. Not only did the Lord not sin; he didn't even use his words to deceive. That's the Serpent's way. With forked tongue, the Devil trades in half-truths and outright lies. He is the Father of Lies, and we have been his children. So observant human beings are stunned when one enters history who committed no sin and never deceived. If we can, we ought to imagine purity from heart to lips, from behavior to speech. Not even reviling and suffering could make him break God's holy law. Jesus was like us in every way, except without sin (Heb. 4:15).

SIN BEARER

Even more stunning than Jesus' perfection—if something could be more stunning—is that "he himself bore our sins in his body on the tree, that we might die to sin and live to righteousness." The one without sin became the one sin bearer.

Ineffable.

Peter makes certain to remind us "he himself bore our sins." In other words, the Lord Jesus did not delegate sin bearing to another. He chose no subordinate to run his holy errand. Angels are ministering spirits sent out for the sake of our salvation (Heb. 1:14). Christ commands legions of angels. Yet Jesus, he himself, personally shouldered the great burden of our sin. The work of redemption belonged uniquely and solely to him. He himself.

THE WORK OF REDEMPTION BELONGED UNIQUELY AND SOLELY TO HIM.

Moreover, the Lord "bore our sins in his body." The carrying of sin was not a fantasy, an intellectual abstraction, or merely a spiritual principle. Rather, sin bearing had physical consequence. As the writer of Hebrews teaches us:

For it is impossible for the blood of bulls and goats to
　　take away sins.
Consequently, when Christ came into the world,
he said, "Sacrifices and offerings you have not desired,
　　but a body have you prepared for me;
in burnt offerings and sin offerings
　　you have taken no pleasure. (10:4–6, ESV)

The Father prepared a body for the Son because other sacrifices and offerings were not desirable. The Father took no
pleasure in them. The temple sacrifices and offerings were but
pointers to another body, a human body, specifically prepared
to bear sin. In this body, broken for us, the Father found pleasure and delight. In that body a new possibility was opened
for us—"that we might die to sin and live to righteousness."
　　But how?

WOUNDED HEALER

"By his wounds you have been healed." The sinless one became
the sin bearer for our healing.

　　Those physical wounds on a rugged cross by God's grace
became the healing agent in our salvation. On the cross, Jesus
Christ became heaven's apothecary, dispensing the one med-
icine our souls desperately needed—his blood.

　　Flesh torn to ribbons by a Roman whip. Head punctured
with the crown of thorns. Metal nails pounded through wrists
and feet. Side lanced with spear. What wounds are these?
Wounds that healed not themselves but others. Wounds that
healed you. How could Jesus be stricken and we be strengthened? How could Jesus be tortured but we be treated? How
could Jesus be harmed so grotesquely but we be healed so
completely? ◾

THE
THINGS
THAT ARE
UNSEEN

By Jared C. Wilson

meditations on

HOLY SATURDAY

████████

2 Corinthians 4:16-18

IN JANUARY 2020, I thought I had a heart attack. I was sitting in my office at the seminary where I work, waiting my turn to speak in chapel to a thousand students attending our annual youth conference. I spoke at the event every year. I was prepared. I was not nervous or worried. Iced coffee in hand, I was simply sitting at my desk, watching the previous speaker on the livestream, casually waiting.

Suddenly I felt my chest tighten and my heart begin to race. The only way I have been able to describe what happened next is that it seemed as if my body was "shutting down." I had the overwhelming feeling that I was about to die.

The next thing I remember thinking is that if I die in my office on a Saturday, nobody would find me for a long time, so I made my way toward the chapel complex where I might be able to get help. I made it as far as a bench in the lobby where I was noticed by one of our security staff, and it was not long before 911 was called, paramedics arrived, and I was being gawked at by hundreds of teenagers who were filing out of the chapel for a break.

I was not rushed to the hospital that day. The paramedics offered, but they determined it wasn't necessary. After several tests and scans that week in a variety of medical facilities, my doctor diagnosed my episode as a "stress-induced panic attack."

OUTWARDLY WE MAY BE WASTING AWAY, BUT INWARDLY WE ARE BEING RENEWED.

This diagnosis wasn't entirely surprising to me. I had been dealing with sporadic episodes of anxiety for years (and still do). But I'd never had an episode that terrifying, that serious. I had not had one that I'd mistaken for a heart attack and felt as though I would die. The other surprising thing about this event was the circumstance of its occurrence. I wasn't doing anything particularly stressful or taxing. In fact, up until that moment, I felt fairly relaxed. I was just hanging out. Just waiting.

Five years later, I have not had any incidents as serious as that one. But I know full well that I'm carrying around in this aging and increasingly tired body the potential for another all-out collapse. There is a dark shadow just lurking right behind me at all times. I have no illusions about my frailty comparing to the kinds of disabilities and diseases with which millions of others suffer on a daily basis. To varying degrees, every person on this broken, cursed earth feels that brokenness, that cursedness in their bones. We all try to medicate against it in different ways. We all try to distract ourselves from the darkness of that shadow. We even try to vanquish it. But try as we might, as far as we might distance ourselves from it, it's always there. It's waiting too.

In 2 Corinthians 4:16-18, the apostle Paul, who knows a little something about carrying brokenness around in his body, encourages believers not to lose heart. Outwardly we may be wasting away, but inwardly we are being renewed. How can he say this, knowing that we can't outwait the shadow of brokenness?

The brokenness will be redeemed. And in fact, the redemption will be so eternally glorious, it will, by contrast, make the brokenness seem like a "light, momentary affliction."

If you think about it, our world this side of heaven is a lifetime of Holy Saturday. Christ has come, and he will come again. But in the meantime, we are waiting. For some, the wait will feel short; for others, it may feel like an eternity. But we can take heart in knowing that the wait isn't forever. And while the shadow of death and brokenness may be waiting for us, it is also waiting for its own end. What we see is just transient. What we can't see is eternal. And for those who trust in Jesus, not even death is eternal.

In his cross, Christ has canceled the debt that stood against us, taking the condemnation we were owed upon himself and removing it forever from us. In his resurrection, Christ emerges victorious over death and hell, holding their keys and purchasing the power of eternal life for all who believe in him. This means that the resurrection of Jesus is the shadow lurking behind death itself! He'll get it before it gets us.

On this Holy Saturday, whatever our ailments, whatever our worries—whatever our circumstances or sins—let us take heart in our waiting. There's an eternal weight of glory coming. And in the end, we will see with the eyes of immortality that it was worth waiting for. ▪

celebration of
EASTER

"Weeping may
tarry for the night,
but joy comes with
the morning."

PSALM 30:5 (ESV)

SWALLOWED UP IN VICTORY

By Malcolm Guite

1 Corinthians 15:53–56

PAUL'S GREAT HYMN OF EASTER VICTORY in 1 Corinthians 15 has resounded down the centuries, encouraging every Christian and inspiring some of the greatest poets. Indeed, in this hymn, Paul himself quotes the poetry of the prophets, specifically Isaiah 25:8 where it is written Christ will swallow up death forever. What was still a prophecy for Isaiah had come gloriously true for the apostle who met the risen Christ on the road to Damascus, and it is going to come gloriously true for every Christian. And even now, thanks to Scripture's witness to the Resurrection, we can taste something of Christ's victory and exalt in it just as Paul does.

"Death has been swallowed up in victory"! There is a powerful paradox here, a great gospel reversal! For until Easter it was death who did all the swallowing, swallowing up every life, every civilization, swallowing up so many hopes and dreams, breaking so many hearts. But now death itself is swallowed up, and it is life, the resurrection life Jesus shares with us, that swallows death and stands triumphant.

Here is how two of the greatest Christian poets have responded to that victory in Christ. The Scottish priest-poet William Dunbar (1460-1530), writing over 500 years ago, celebrated Christ's Easter triumph (you can surely hear his joy even through his archaic Scots dialect):

Done is a battle on the dragon black,
Our champion Christ confoundit has his force;
The yetis [gates] of hell are broken with a crack,
The sign triumphal raisit is of the cross.

Those are the opening lines of his poem, and for Dunbar it is not only death that has been defeated but the devil himself, "that old dragon," and the gates of hell have been cracked right open!

Every verse of this poems ends with a proclamation of resurrection, and the third verse gets right to the heart of the matter:

He for our saik that sufferit to be slane,
And lyk a lamb in sacrifice was dicht,
Is lyk a lion risen up agane.

THANKS TO THE SCRIPTURE'S WITNESS TO THE RESURRECTION, WE CAN TASTE SOMETHING OF CHRIST'S VICTORY AND EXALT IN IT JUST AS PAUL DOES.

The one who allowed himself to be slain for our sake, who was sacrificed as a lamb, now rises like a lion! As a medieval scholar, C. S. Lewis knew and loved this poem, and I sometimes wonder if it gave him an idea for a story!

More than a century later another priest-poet, the Englishman John Donne, took inspiration from this same victory hymn in 1 Corinthians for his great sonnet "Death Be Not Proud." Just as Paul writes, "O death, where is thy sting?" (1 Cor. 15:55, KJV), so Donne follows Paul's example in addressing death directly, and, as Paul does, openly taunting death. He turns the tables on death, and instead of living in fear or cowering at the prospect of death, he stands up and mocks him, reminding him that he himself will die when death is swallowed up in victory. The poem opens with a bold rebuke:

> Death, be not proud, though some have called thee
> Mighty and dreadful, for thou art not so;
> For those whom thou think'st thou dost overthrow
> Die not, poor Death, nor yet canst thou kill me.

Donne goes on to compare death to sleep, preparing us for the beautiful image of waking to resurrection, which will come at the end of the poem:

> From rest and sleep, which but thy pictures be,
> Much pleasure; then from thee much more must flow,
> And soonest our best men with thee do go,
> Rest of their bones, and soul's delivery.

Donne continues by telling death that he is merely a servant, indeed a "slave to fate, chance, kings, and desperate men," and then comes the triumphant final couplet, two of the most famous lines in English poetry, lines which have given courage and peace in the face of death to so many:

> One short sleep past, we wake eternally
> And death shall be no more; Death, thou shalt die.

May we all rest and rise in the good news of Easter, the news that "one short sleep past, we wake eternally."

WHY DO DOUBTS ARISE?

By Jeremy Writebol

celebrations of

EASTER MONDAY

━━━━━━━━

Luke 24:36–49

HOW DO YOU IMAGINE Jesus' attitude and posture are toward you right now? Is he annoyed, bothered that here you are again, not having it all together, asking questions? Is he absent, not even present to address your despair or desire? Maybe you perceive Jesus as apathetic about you. You're really not high (if at all) on his list of most interesting people or situations to engage. I wonder if you think Jesus is angry with you right now. You know he knows what you've done. You both are intimately aware of your sinful heart, and Jesus is furious with you. He's not having any of it.

So here you are on Easter Monday, and while maybe there is a modicum of joy from yesterday's celebrations, you are still apprehensive about Jesus' intentions and interest in you. You can celebrate that, yes, "He is risen!" but that nagging doubt in the back of your heart still creeps forward, making you wonder if that really is a good thing, if it really matters, if Jesus is positively for you.

These kinds of doubts and anxious thoughts are not new to us. Nor are they new to the experience of Easter. Jesus' own disciples carried troubled hearts, doubt-filled minds, astonished and overwhelmed emotions, and big questions. The resurrection of Jesus from the dead called out the deepest concern: *Now what!* Everything was on the table. From Judas's denial, Peter's betrayal, the other nine's withdrawal, and only John being faithful, what would Jesus' posture to them be now?

WHEN THE MOMENT ARISES WHERE JESUS COULD BE UTTERLY ANNOYED BY THEIR DEFICIENCY OF FAITH, HE AGAIN INCLINES HIMSELF TO ANSWER THEIR LACK OF UNDERSTANDING.

The words and actions of Jesus in Luke 24:36-49 must inform and override our perhaps skewed perspectives. Instead of absence, Jesus is present. He shows up and draws near to his friends. Instead of anger and volatility toward this mutinous crew, Jesus pronounces peace and reconciliation. He's not frothing at the bit to bring down the hammer of justice. Instead of being apathetic about their worries and anxieties, Jesus is curious. He asks why they are troubled, and then avails himself to their inquiries by giving tangible evidence of his physical resurrection. When the moment arises where Jesus could be utterly annoyed by their deficiency of faith, he again inclines himself to answer their lack of understanding. In every turn of this story that could prove to be the final repellent of Jesus away from his followers, he instead draws close.

If we are not careful, we can too quickly read through this narrative as if it is a rational or logical apologetic text proving the historicity of the Resurrection. We can miss that this is a relational drama demonstrating the heart of Jesus toward anxious and doubtful people like you and me. We're given this vignette into Jesus' relationship with his disciples so that we can be encouraged about his relationship to us today.

Easter Monday might not bring any of the joy or bliss that Easter Sunday did. We're glad that Lent is over, thankful Jesus is proclaimed alive, but we have our lives to get on with. And there we wonder, *How is Jesus going to think of us today?*

The events of Good Friday, Holy Saturday, and Resurrection Sunday incline us to embrace Jesus' victory over the cosmic realms of Satan, sin, and death. They tell us of an ascending king enthroned, establishing, and emerging with his kingdom. They tell us of a sacrificial Savior who died for the sins of the world and was raised to life again "for us and for our salvation" (Nicene Creed). Easter Monday brings us the assurance that Jesus hasn't overlooked or been indifferent to us. He brings his affection and love right to our very individual and personal needs.

Easter Monday is a place for us to stop and reflect, *What is Jesus' attitude and posture toward me?* Today is a waypoint in our journey to be reacquainted with the Savior who personally knows, sees, and loves us. He bears no hostility, indifference, or ignorance of our doubts and needs. He only is inclined in love to our frailty and feebleness. Furthermore, he loves to be the Good Shepherd who knows and cares for his sheep. You can draw really close to him today because he's already moved close to you!

WHO FOR THE JOY SET BEFORE HIM

By Kristie Anyabwile

Hebrews 12:1–2

"**THEREFORE, SINCE WE** are surrounded by so great a cloud of witnesses, let us also lay aside every weight, and sin which clings so closely, and let us run with endurance the race that is set before us, looking to Jesus, the founder and perfecter of our faith, who for the joy that was set before him endured the cross, despising the shame, and is seated at the right hand of the throne of God" (Heb. 12:1–2, ESV).

Many of us get annoyed when someone constantly asks on a trip, "Are we there yet?" This question not only makes the trip seem to take forever, but it also shows discontentment and failure to evaluate time, place, and space on your own. On the other hand, there's almost no sweeter sound than hearing the driver say, "We're here," or the pilot announcing, "We are on our final descent. We should land at our destination shortly."

Just as travelers longs to reach their destination, the faithful in ages past yearned for the fulfillment of God's promises. Hebrews 12:1-2 ends a long encomium on faith that started in Hebrews 11:1. Faith is the virtue that is praised in saints of old. The people of Israel, the faithful witnesses and prophets, looked forward to the Messiah, asking "what person or time the Spirit of Christ in them was indicating when he predicted the sufferings of Christ and the subsequent glories" (1 Pet. 1:10-11, ESV). Their faith rested in the Spirit's testimony of the coming sufferings and glories of Christ. They rightly wanted to know "Who is he?" and "When is he coming?" It was their version of "Are we there yet?" They walked in faith, looking forward to the coming Messiah. We look back to our crucified and risen Savior, who left glory to come in the likeness of sinful humanity and for the sins of humanity, to condemn sin in the flesh so that "the righteous requirement of the law might be fulfilled in us, who walk not according to the flesh but according to the Spirit" (Rom. 8:3-4, ESV).

BY FAITH, WE IMITATE HIS JOYFUL ENDURANCE OF SUFFERING IN ANTICIPATION OF OUR FUTURE REIGN WITH HIM IN GLORY.

As we look back on the cloud of witnesses, we see men and women who made the choice to obey God even when everyone and everything around them and in them would have encouraged them to go another way, make a different decision. However, Jesus says that his yoke is easy and his burden is light, not because the road we travel or the task we undertake is light, but because the finish line is in our view. We don't carry the heavy load; Jesus carries it for us. I'm reminded of a line in an old song that my dad used to play on his eight-track player when I was a kid. The line goes, "Heavy load. Heavy load. God's gonna lighten up my heavy load." This song echoes the truth that Jesus took upon himself the weight and shame and guilt of sin as well as the punishment for sin. "He himself bore our sins in his body on the tree, that we might die to sin and live to righteousness" (1 Pet. 2:24, ESV). Jesus found joy in enduring the cross, despite its pain and humiliation, and disregarded its shame to become sin for us. Why? So that through his substitutionary, atoning death, he might declare us righteous before the Father. Having completed the work God sent him to do, Jesus now sits at the right hand of God, always interceding for us. If dying for us brought him such joy, shouldn't living for him bring us joy?

During Lent, we have a unique opportunity to imitate Jesus. By faith, we imitate his joyful endurance of suffering in anticipation of our future reign with him in glory. The faithful witnesses endured and walked in faith despite their circumstances. They waited in faith because they looked not at their present circumstances, but ahead toward God's promise of a future homeland, the city that he had prepared for them. They, and believers today, know that our true destination is not a city built by human hands, but a home whose builder and designer is God (Heb. 11:10).

Unlike us, Jesus is not annoyed by our "Are we there yet?" question. Through the Cross, Jesus answers, "I will have you at your final destination shortly." The journey to our true home is cross-shaped and joy-filled. Through Christ's example, we learn that the journey to our eternal home is paved with the promise of unshakable joy in the glory that awaits us. ■

Contributors

KRISTIE ANYABWILE
Kristie Anyabwile is a Bible teacher and author of several books, including *Delighting in God's Law: Old Testament Commands and Why They Matter Today*. Her husband, Thabiti, is a pastor in Washington, DC, and they have three adult children.

THABITI ANYABWILE
Thabiti Anyabwile serves as a pastor at Anacostia River Church in Washington, DC, and as president of The Crete Collective. The author of several books, he's happily married to Kristie and is the pleased father of three adult children.

ZACK ESWINE
Zack Eswine (Rev. PhD), serves as lead pastor of Riverside Church in Missouri. His books include *The Imperfect Pastor* and *Wiser with Jesus*. He writes at The Good Dark (thegooddark.substack.com) and is cofounder of Sage Christianity with wife Jessica.

MALCOLM GUITE
Malcolm Guite is a poet, priest, and life fellow of Girton College, Cambridge. His books include *Sounding the Seasons: Seventy Sonnets for the Christian Year* (Canterbury 2012) and *Mariner: A Voyage with Samuel Taylor Coleridge* (Hodder 2017).

DAN HYUN

Dan Hyun finds joy in equipping the church to experience God's presence in cultivating a deeper passion for reconciliation, justice, and mission. He is the founding pastor of The Village Church in Baltimore and author of *The Bible in 52 Weeks*.

JEREMY LINNEMAN

Jeremy Linneman (DMin Covenant Theological Seminary) serves as lead pastor of Trinity Community Church in Columbia, Missouri. He's the author of *Pour Out Your Heart: Discovering Joy, Strength, and Intimacy with God through Prayer*. Jeremy and his wife, Jessie, have three sons.

RAY ORTLUND

Pastor Ray Ortlund is the president of Renewal Ministries and a canon theologian in the Anglican Church in North America. Ortlund graduated from University of Aberdeen (PhD), and was ordained into Christian ministry by Lake Avenue Church, Pasadena, in 1975.

BARNABAS PIPER

Barnabas Piper serves as a pastor at Immanuel Church in Nashville. He is the author of *The Pastor's Kid* and *Belong*. He is married to his wife, Lauren, and has three children.

JOHN STARKE

John Starke is lead pastor of Apostles Church Uptown and lives with his wife, Jena, and their four children in New York City. He is the author of *The Possibility of Prayer* (IVP) and *The Secret Place of Thunder* (Zondervan).

HEATHER THOMPSON DAY

Heather Thompson Day, PhD, is the founder of It Is Day Ministries, a nonprofit organization that trains churches, leaders, and laypeople with a gospel-centered communication approach. She has authored nine books, including *I'll See You Tomorrow* and *What If I'm Wrong?*

EVAN WELCHER

Evan Welcher is a pastor of Grace Baptsist Church, Vermillion, South Dakota, and the author of *Advent: A Thread in the Night*, *Nightscapes: Poetry from the Depths*, and *Resplendent Bride: Essays on Love & Loss*.

JAMAAL WILLIAMS

Jamaal Williams is lead pastor of Sojourn Church Midtown in Louisville, Kentucky, and president of Harbor Network. He is the coauthor of *In Church as It Is in Heaven*. Jamaal lives in Louisville with his wife, Amber, and their five children.

JARED C. WILSON

Jared C. Wilson is assistant professor of pastoral ministry at Midwestern Seminary and pastor for preaching at Liberty Baptist Church in Liberty, Missouri. He is the author of *Friendship with the Friend of Sinners* and cohost of *The Heart of Pastoring Podcast*.

JEREMY WRITEBOL

Jeremy Writebol serves as lead campus pastor at Woodside Bible Church in Plymouth, Michigan, and is executive director of Gospel-Centered Discipleship. He has authored several books including *Pastor, Jesus Is Enough*. He is married to Stephanie and has two children.